50 Casserole Classic Recipes for Home

By: Kelly Johnson

Table of Contents

- Green Bean Casserole
- Tuna Noodle Casserole
- Chicken and Rice Casserole
- Beef Stroganoff Casserole
- Baked Ziti
- Cheesy Broccoli and Rice Casserole
- Shepherd's Pie
- Macaroni and Cheese Casserole
- Lasagna
- Potato and Ham Casserole
- Vegetable Lasagna
- Egg and Sausage Breakfast Casserole
- Chicken Enchilada Casserole
- Stuffed Pepper Casserole
- Sweet Potato Casserole
- Ratatouille Casserole
- Pizza Casserole
- Quinoa and Black Bean Casserole
- Chili Mac Casserole
- Seafood Casserole
- Baked Chicken Parmesan Casserole
- Sloppy Joe Casserole
- Cabbage Roll Casserole
- Eggplant Parmesan Casserole
- Pasta Primavera Casserole
- Cornbread Casserole
- Curry Chicken Casserole
- French Onion Soup Casserole
- BBQ Chicken Casserole
- Cheesy Cauliflower Casserole
- Ham and Cheese Breakfast Casserole
- Creamy Mushroom Casserole
- Zucchini and Tomato Casserole
- Stuffed Cabbage Casserole

- Mushroom and Rice Casserole
- Buffalo Chicken Casserole
- Lentil and Vegetable Casserole
- Chili Cheese Dog Casserole
- Southwestern Quinoa Casserole
- Meatball Casserole
- Potato Topping Casserole
- Savory Breakfast Casserole
- Baked Ratatouille Casserole
- Crab and Corn Casserole
- Pasta Fagioli Casserole
- Herbed Chicken and Potato Casserole
- Cranberry Chicken Casserole
- Crispy Tater Tot Casserole
- Bacon and Egg Casserole
- Mediterranean Vegetable Casserole

Classic Green Bean Casserole

Ingredients

For the Casserole:

- 1 (16 oz) can of cut green beans (or 2 cups fresh or frozen green beans, trimmed and blanched)
- 1 (10.5 oz) can of condensed cream of mushroom soup
- ½ cup milk
- 1 cup shredded cheddar cheese (optional)
- 1 teaspoon soy sauce
- 1 cup crispy fried onions (divided)

Instructions

1. **Preheat Oven:** Preheat your oven to 350°F (175°C).
2. **Mix Ingredients:** In a large mixing bowl, combine the green beans, cream of mushroom soup, milk, soy sauce, and half of the crispy fried onions. If using, add the cheddar cheese and mix well.
3. **Transfer to Baking Dish:** Pour the mixture into a greased 1.5-quart casserole dish and spread it evenly.
4. **Bake:** Bake in the preheated oven for about 25 minutes, or until the mixture is hot and bubbly.
5. **Add Topping:** Remove the casserole from the oven, sprinkle the remaining fried onions on top, and return it to the oven.
6. **Final Bake:** Bake for an additional 10-15 minutes, or until the onions are golden brown.
7. **Serve:** Let it cool for a few minutes before serving. Enjoy!

Tuna Noodle Casserole

Ingredients

For the Casserole:

- 1 (12 oz) package of egg noodles
- 1 (10.5 oz) can of condensed cream of mushroom soup
- 1 cup milk
- 2 (5 oz) cans of tuna, drained
- 1 cup frozen peas
- 1 cup shredded cheddar cheese (divided)
- 1 teaspoon garlic powder
- 1 cup crushed potato chips (optional)

Instructions

1. **Preheat Oven:** Preheat your oven to 350°F (175°C).
2. **Cook Noodles:** Cook the egg noodles according to package instructions; drain and set aside.
3. **Mix Ingredients:** In a large mixing bowl, combine the cream of mushroom soup, milk, tuna, peas, garlic powder, and half of the cheddar cheese. Mix well.
4. **Combine Noodles:** Fold the cooked noodles into the mixture until well combined.
5. **Transfer to Baking Dish:** Pour the mixture into a greased 2-quart casserole dish and spread it evenly.
6. **Add Topping:** Sprinkle the remaining cheddar cheese and crushed potato chips on top.
7. **Bake:** Bake in the preheated oven for 25-30 minutes, or until the casserole is hot and bubbly.
8. **Serve:** Let it cool for a few minutes before serving. Enjoy!

Chicken and Rice Casserole

Ingredients

For the Casserole:

- 2 cups cooked rice
- 2 cups cooked chicken, shredded
- 1 (10.5 oz) can of condensed cream of chicken soup
- 1 cup milk
- 1 cup frozen mixed vegetables
- 1 teaspoon onion powder
- 1 cup shredded cheddar cheese (divided)

Instructions

1. **Preheat Oven:** Preheat your oven to 350°F (175°C).
2. **Mix Ingredients:** In a large mixing bowl, combine the cooked rice, shredded chicken, cream of chicken soup, milk, mixed vegetables, onion powder, and half of the cheddar cheese. Mix well.
3. **Transfer to Baking Dish:** Pour the mixture into a greased 2-quart casserole dish and spread it evenly.
4. **Add Topping:** Sprinkle the remaining cheddar cheese on top.
5. **Bake:** Bake in the preheated oven for 30-35 minutes, or until heated through.
6. **Serve:** Let it cool for a few minutes before serving. Enjoy!

Beef Stroganoff Casserole

Ingredients

For the Casserole:

- 1 (12 oz) package of egg noodles
- 1 lb ground beef
- 1 (10.5 oz) can of condensed cream of mushroom soup
- 1 cup sour cream
- 1 medium onion, chopped
- 1 cup sliced mushrooms
- 1 teaspoon Worcestershire sauce
- 1 cup shredded cheddar cheese (optional)

Instructions

1. **Preheat Oven:** Preheat your oven to 350°F (175°C).
2. **Cook Noodles:** Cook the egg noodles according to package instructions; drain and set aside.
3. **Brown Beef:** In a skillet, brown the ground beef and onion until the beef is cooked through. Drain excess fat.
4. **Mix Ingredients:** Stir in the mushrooms, cream of mushroom soup, sour cream, Worcestershire sauce, and cooked noodles. Mix well.
5. **Transfer to Baking Dish:** Pour the mixture into a greased 2-quart casserole dish and spread it evenly.
6. **Add Topping:** If desired, sprinkle cheddar cheese on top.
7. **Bake:** Bake in the preheated oven for 25-30 minutes, or until hot and bubbly.
8. **Serve:** Let it cool for a few minutes before serving. Enjoy!

Baked Ziti

Ingredients

For the Casserole:

- 1 lb ziti pasta
- 2 cups marinara sauce
- 2 cups ricotta cheese
- 1 egg
- 2 cups shredded mozzarella cheese (divided)
- 1 teaspoon Italian seasoning
- ½ cup grated Parmesan cheese

Instructions

1. **Preheat Oven:** Preheat your oven to 350°F (175°C).
2. **Cook Pasta:** Cook the ziti according to package instructions; drain and set aside.
3. **Mix Ingredients:** In a large bowl, combine marinara sauce, ricotta cheese, egg, Italian seasoning, and half of the mozzarella cheese. Mix well.
4. **Combine Pasta:** Fold the cooked ziti into the cheese mixture until well combined.
5. **Transfer to Baking Dish:** Pour the mixture into a greased 3-quart baking dish and spread evenly.
6. **Add Topping:** Sprinkle the remaining mozzarella and Parmesan cheese on top.
7. **Bake:** Bake in the preheated oven for 30-35 minutes, or until cheese is bubbly and golden.
8. **Serve:** Let it cool for a few minutes before serving. Enjoy!

Cheesy Broccoli and Rice Casserole

Ingredients

For the Casserole:

- 2 cups cooked rice
- 2 cups broccoli florets (fresh or frozen)
- 1 (10.5 oz) can of condensed cream of mushroom soup
- 1 cup milk
- 1 cup shredded cheddar cheese (divided)
- 1 teaspoon garlic powder

Instructions

1. **Preheat Oven:** Preheat your oven to 350°F (175°C).
2. **Mix Ingredients:** In a large mixing bowl, combine cooked rice, broccoli, cream of mushroom soup, milk, garlic powder, and half of the cheddar cheese. Mix well.
3. **Transfer to Baking Dish:** Pour the mixture into a greased 2-quart casserole dish and spread it evenly.
4. **Add Topping:** Sprinkle the remaining cheddar cheese on top.
5. **Bake:** Bake in the preheated oven for 25-30 minutes, or until heated through and cheese is melted.
6. **Serve:** Let it cool for a few minutes before serving. Enjoy!

Shepherd's Pie

Ingredients

For the Casserole:

- 1 lb ground beef or lamb
- 1 cup frozen mixed vegetables
- 1 (10.5 oz) can of condensed cream of mushroom soup
- 1 teaspoon Worcestershire sauce
- 4 cups mashed potatoes (prepared)
- 1 cup shredded cheddar cheese (optional)

Instructions

1. **Preheat Oven:** Preheat your oven to 350°F (175°C).
2. **Brown Meat:** In a skillet, cook the ground beef or lamb until browned. Drain excess fat.
3. **Mix Ingredients:** Stir in the mixed vegetables, cream of mushroom soup, and Worcestershire sauce. Mix well.
4. **Transfer to Baking Dish:** Pour the meat mixture into a greased 2-quart baking dish and spread it evenly.
5. **Add Potatoes:** Spread the mashed potatoes over the meat mixture, smoothing it out. If desired, sprinkle cheddar cheese on top.
6. **Bake:** Bake in the preheated oven for 25-30 minutes, or until the potatoes are golden.
7. **Serve:** Let it cool for a few minutes before serving. Enjoy!

Macaroni and Cheese Casserole

Ingredients

For the Casserole:

- 1 lb elbow macaroni
- 4 cups shredded sharp cheddar cheese (divided)
- 1 (12 oz) can evaporated milk
- 1 cup milk
- 2 large eggs
- ½ teaspoon garlic powder
- ½ teaspoon onion powder
- 1 teaspoon salt
- ½ teaspoon black pepper

Instructions

1. **Preheat Oven:** Preheat your oven to 350°F (175°C).
2. **Cook Macaroni:** Cook the macaroni according to package instructions; drain and set aside.
3. **Mix Ingredients:** In a large bowl, whisk together evaporated milk, milk, eggs, garlic powder, onion powder, salt, and pepper.
4. **Combine Mixture:** Stir in the cooked macaroni and 3 cups of the cheese until well combined.
5. **Transfer to Baking Dish:** Pour the mixture into a greased 3-quart casserole dish and spread evenly.
6. **Add Topping:** Sprinkle the remaining cheese on top.
7. **Bake:** Bake in the preheated oven for 30-35 minutes, or until the cheese is bubbly and golden.
8. **Serve:** Let it cool for a few minutes before serving. Enjoy!

Lasagna

Ingredients
For the Casserole:

- 12 lasagna noodles
- 1 lb ground beef
- 1 (26 oz) jar marinara sauce
- 15 oz ricotta cheese
- 1 cup grated Parmesan cheese
- 2 cups shredded mozzarella cheese (divided)
- 1 egg
- 1 teaspoon Italian seasoning

Instructions

1. **Preheat Oven:** Preheat your oven to 375°F (190°C).
2. **Cook Noodles:** Cook the lasagna noodles according to package instructions; drain and set aside.
3. **Brown Beef:** In a skillet, brown the ground beef; drain excess fat. Stir in marinara sauce and simmer for a few minutes.
4. **Mix Cheese Filling:** In a bowl, combine ricotta cheese, egg, Parmesan cheese, and Italian seasoning. Mix well.
5. **Layer Ingredients:** Spread a thin layer of meat sauce in a greased 9x13-inch baking dish. Layer 4 noodles, half of the ricotta mixture, a third of the mozzarella, and a third of the meat sauce. Repeat layers, ending with noodles and remaining meat sauce. Top with remaining mozzarella.
6. **Bake:** Cover with foil and bake for 25 minutes. Remove foil and bake for an additional 15-20 minutes, or until cheese is melted and bubbly.
7. **Serve:** Let it cool for a few minutes before serving. Enjoy!

Potato and Ham Casserole

Ingredients

For the Casserole:

- 4 cups diced potatoes (fresh or frozen)
- 2 cups diced ham
- 1 (10.5 oz) can of condensed cream of mushroom soup
- 1 cup milk
- 1 cup shredded cheddar cheese (divided)
- 1 teaspoon garlic powder
- ½ teaspoon black pepper

Instructions

1. **Preheat Oven:** Preheat your oven to 350°F (175°C).
2. **Mix Ingredients:** In a large bowl, combine potatoes, ham, cream of mushroom soup, milk, garlic powder, and black pepper. Mix well.
3. **Transfer to Baking Dish:** Pour the mixture into a greased 2-quart casserole dish and spread it evenly.
4. **Add Topping:** Sprinkle half of the cheddar cheese on top.
5. **Bake:** Cover with foil and bake for 45 minutes. Remove foil, add remaining cheese, and bake for an additional 15 minutes, or until potatoes are tender and cheese is melted.
6. **Serve:** Let it cool for a few minutes before serving. Enjoy!

Vegetable Lasagna

Ingredients

For the Casserole:

- 12 lasagna noodles
- 1 (26 oz) jar marinara sauce
- 2 cups chopped spinach (fresh or frozen)
- 1 cup sliced mushrooms
- 1 zucchini, sliced
- 15 oz ricotta cheese
- 2 cups shredded mozzarella cheese (divided)
- 1 cup grated Parmesan cheese
- 1 egg
- 1 teaspoon Italian seasoning

Instructions

1. **Preheat Oven:** Preheat your oven to 375°F (190°C).
2. **Cook Noodles:** Cook the lasagna noodles according to package instructions; drain and set aside.
3. **Mix Cheese Filling:** In a bowl, combine ricotta cheese, egg, Parmesan cheese, and Italian seasoning. Mix well.
4. **Layer Ingredients:** Spread a thin layer of marinara sauce in a greased 9x13-inch baking dish. Layer 4 noodles, half of the ricotta mixture, half of the spinach, half of the mushrooms, half of the zucchini, and a third of the marinara sauce. Repeat layers, ending with noodles and remaining marinara sauce. Top with remaining mozzarella.
5. **Bake:** Cover with foil and bake for 30 minutes. Remove foil and bake for an additional 15-20 minutes, or until cheese is melted and bubbly.
6. **Serve:** Let it cool for a few minutes before serving. Enjoy!

Egg and Sausage Breakfast Casserole

Ingredients

For the Casserole:

- 1 lb breakfast sausage
- 6 large eggs
- 2 cups milk
- 1 cup shredded cheddar cheese
- 1 cup diced bell peppers
- 1 cup diced onion
- 1 teaspoon salt
- ½ teaspoon black pepper
- 6 slices of bread, cubed

Instructions

1. **Preheat Oven:** Preheat your oven to 350°F (175°C).
2. **Brown Sausage:** In a skillet, cook the sausage over medium heat until browned. Drain excess fat.
3. **Mix Ingredients:** In a large bowl, whisk together eggs, milk, salt, and pepper. Stir in the cooked sausage, cheese, bell peppers, onions, and cubed bread.
4. **Transfer to Baking Dish:** Pour the mixture into a greased 9x13-inch baking dish and spread evenly.
5. **Bake:** Bake in the preheated oven for 30-35 minutes, or until the center is set and the top is golden.
6. **Serve:** Let it cool for a few minutes before serving. Enjoy!

Chicken Enchilada Casserole

Ingredients

For the Casserole:

- 3 cups cooked chicken, shredded
- 2 cups enchilada sauce
- 1 cup black beans, drained and rinsed
- 1 cup corn
- 1 cup diced bell peppers
- 1 teaspoon cumin
- 1 cup shredded cheddar cheese (divided)
- 8 corn tortillas, cut into strips

Instructions

1. **Preheat Oven:** Preheat your oven to 350°F (175°C).
2. **Mix Ingredients:** In a large bowl, combine shredded chicken, enchilada sauce, black beans, corn, bell peppers, cumin, and half of the cheddar cheese. Mix well.
3. **Layer Ingredients:** Spread a thin layer of the chicken mixture in a greased 9x13-inch baking dish. Layer half of the tortilla strips, followed by half of the remaining chicken mixture, and repeat layers. Top with remaining cheese.
4. **Bake:** Bake in the preheated oven for 25-30 minutes, or until hot and bubbly.
5. **Serve:** Let it cool for a few minutes before serving. Enjoy!

Stuffed Pepper Casserole

Ingredients

For the Casserole:

- 1 lb ground beef
- 1 cup diced bell peppers
- 1 cup diced onion
- 1 (14.5 oz) can diced tomatoes
- 1 cup cooked rice
- 1 teaspoon Italian seasoning
- 1 cup shredded mozzarella cheese (divided)
- ½ teaspoon salt
- ½ teaspoon black pepper

Instructions

1. **Preheat Oven:** Preheat your oven to 350°F (175°C).
2. **Brown Meat:** In a skillet, cook the ground beef, bell peppers, and onion until the beef is browned. Drain excess fat.
3. **Mix Ingredients:** Stir in diced tomatoes, cooked rice, Italian seasoning, salt, and pepper. Mix well.
4. **Transfer to Baking Dish:** Pour the mixture into a greased 2-quart casserole dish and spread evenly.
5. **Add Topping:** Sprinkle half of the mozzarella cheese on top.
6. **Bake:** Bake in the preheated oven for 25-30 minutes. Add remaining cheese and bake for an additional 5-10 minutes, or until cheese is melted.
7. **Serve:** Let it cool for a few minutes before serving. Enjoy!

Sweet Potato Casserole

Ingredients

For the Casserole:

- 4 cups mashed sweet potatoes (about 4 large sweet potatoes)
- ½ cup brown sugar
- ½ cup milk
- 1 teaspoon vanilla extract
- 1 teaspoon cinnamon
- 2 large eggs, beaten
- 1 cup mini marshmallows (optional)

Instructions

1. **Preheat Oven:** Preheat your oven to 350°F (175°C).
2. **Mix Ingredients:** In a large bowl, combine mashed sweet potatoes, brown sugar, milk, vanilla extract, cinnamon, and beaten eggs. Mix until smooth.
3. **Transfer to Baking Dish:** Pour the mixture into a greased 2-quart casserole dish and spread evenly.
4. **Add Topping:** If desired, sprinkle mini marshmallows on top.
5. **Bake:** Bake in the preheated oven for 30-35 minutes, or until heated through and marshmallows are golden.
6. **Serve:** Let it cool for a few minutes before serving. Enjoy!

Ratatouille Casserole

Ingredients

For the Casserole:

- 1 medium eggplant, diced
- 2 medium zucchini, sliced
- 1 bell pepper, diced
- 1 onion, chopped
- 2 cups diced tomatoes (canned or fresh)
- 2 cloves garlic, minced
- 1 teaspoon Italian seasoning
- 1 cup shredded mozzarella cheese (optional)
- Salt and pepper to taste

Instructions

1. **Preheat Oven:** Preheat your oven to 375°F (190°C).
2. **Cook Vegetables:** In a skillet, sauté eggplant, zucchini, bell pepper, onion, and garlic until tender. Season with Italian seasoning, salt, and pepper.
3. **Mix Ingredients:** In a large bowl, combine the sautéed vegetables and diced tomatoes.
4. **Transfer to Baking Dish:** Pour the mixture into a greased 2-quart casserole dish.
5. **Add Topping:** If desired, sprinkle mozzarella cheese on top.
6. **Bake:** Bake in the preheated oven for 25-30 minutes, or until heated through.
7. **Serve:** Let it cool for a few minutes before serving. Enjoy!

Pizza Casserole

Ingredients

For the Casserole:

- 1 lb ground beef or Italian sausage
- 1 (16 oz) package of rotini or penne pasta
- 1 (14 oz) jar pizza sauce
- 1 cup sliced pepperoni
- 2 cups shredded mozzarella cheese (divided)
- 1 teaspoon Italian seasoning
- ½ teaspoon garlic powder

Instructions

1. **Preheat Oven:** Preheat your oven to 350°F (175°C).
2. **Cook Pasta:** Cook the pasta according to package instructions; drain and set aside.
3. **Brown Meat:** In a skillet, cook the ground beef or sausage until browned. Drain excess fat.
4. **Mix Ingredients:** In a large bowl, combine cooked pasta, meat, pizza sauce, pepperoni, Italian seasoning, garlic powder, and half of the mozzarella cheese. Mix well.
5. **Transfer to Baking Dish:** Pour the mixture into a greased 9x13-inch baking dish and spread evenly.
6. **Add Topping:** Sprinkle the remaining mozzarella cheese on top.
7. **Bake:** Bake in the preheated oven for 25-30 minutes, or until cheese is bubbly and golden.
8. **Serve:** Let it cool for a few minutes before serving. Enjoy!

Quinoa and Black Bean Casserole

Ingredients

For the Casserole:

- 1 cup quinoa, rinsed
- 2 cups vegetable broth
- 1 (15 oz) can black beans, drained and rinsed
- 1 cup corn (fresh, frozen, or canned)
- 1 cup diced tomatoes (canned or fresh)
- 1 teaspoon cumin
- 1 teaspoon chili powder
- 1 cup shredded cheddar cheese (optional)

Instructions

1. **Preheat Oven:** Preheat your oven to 350°F (175°C).
2. **Cook Quinoa:** In a saucepan, combine quinoa and vegetable broth. Bring to a boil, then reduce heat, cover, and simmer for 15 minutes.
3. **Mix Ingredients:** In a large bowl, combine cooked quinoa, black beans, corn, diced tomatoes, cumin, chili powder, and half of the cheddar cheese. Mix well.
4. **Transfer to Baking Dish:** Pour the mixture into a greased 2-quart casserole dish and spread evenly.
5. **Add Topping:** Sprinkle the remaining cheese on top.
6. **Bake:** Bake in the preheated oven for 25-30 minutes, or until heated through.
7. **Serve:** Let it cool for a few minutes before serving. Enjoy!

Chili Mac Casserole

Ingredients

For the Casserole:

- 1 lb ground beef
- 1 (16 oz) package elbow macaroni
- 1 (15 oz) can chili (with or without beans)
- 1 (14.5 oz) can diced tomatoes
- 1 cup shredded cheddar cheese (divided)
- 1 teaspoon cumin
- ½ teaspoon garlic powder

Instructions

1. **Preheat Oven:** Preheat your oven to 350°F (175°C).
2. **Cook Pasta:** Cook the macaroni according to package instructions; drain and set aside.
3. **Brown Meat:** In a skillet, cook the ground beef until browned. Drain excess fat.
4. **Mix Ingredients:** In a large bowl, combine cooked macaroni, chili, diced tomatoes, cumin, garlic powder, and half of the cheddar cheese. Mix well.
5. **Transfer to Baking Dish:** Pour the mixture into a greased 2-quart casserole dish and spread evenly.
6. **Add Topping:** Sprinkle the remaining cheddar cheese on top.
7. **Bake:** Bake in the preheated oven for 25-30 minutes, or until hot and bubbly.
8. **Serve:** Let it cool for a few minutes before serving. Enjoy!

Seafood Casserole

Ingredients

For the Casserole:

- 1 lb mixed seafood (shrimp, crab, or scallops)
- 1 (10.5 oz) can of condensed cream of mushroom soup
- 1 cup milk
- 2 cups cooked rice
- 1 cup shredded cheddar cheese (divided)
- 1 teaspoon Old Bay seasoning
- 1 cup crushed crackers (for topping)

Instructions

1. **Preheat Oven:** Preheat your oven to 350°F (175°C).
2. **Mix Ingredients:** In a large bowl, combine seafood, cream of mushroom soup, milk, cooked rice, Old Bay seasoning, and half of the cheddar cheese. Mix well.
3. **Transfer to Baking Dish:** Pour the mixture into a greased 2-quart casserole dish and spread evenly.
4. **Add Topping:** Sprinkle crushed crackers and remaining cheese on top.
5. **Bake:** Bake in the preheated oven for 25-30 minutes, or until hot and bubbly.
6. **Serve:** Let it cool for a few minutes before serving. Enjoy!

Baked Chicken Parmesan Casserole

Ingredients
For the Casserole:

- 2 cups cooked chicken, shredded
- 1 (24 oz) jar marinara sauce
- 2 cups cooked pasta (penne or rotini)
- 1 cup shredded mozzarella cheese (divided)
- ½ cup grated Parmesan cheese
- 1 teaspoon Italian seasoning
- ½ teaspoon garlic powder

Instructions

1. **Preheat Oven:** Preheat your oven to 350°F (175°C).
2. **Mix Ingredients:** In a large bowl, combine shredded chicken, marinara sauce, cooked pasta, Italian seasoning, garlic powder, and half of the mozzarella cheese. Mix well.
3. **Transfer to Baking Dish:** Pour the mixture into a greased 9x13-inch baking dish and spread evenly.
4. **Add Topping:** Sprinkle the remaining mozzarella cheese and Parmesan cheese on top.
5. **Bake:** Bake in the preheated oven for 25-30 minutes, or until cheese is melted and bubbly.
6. **Serve:** Let it cool for a few minutes before serving. Enjoy!

Sloppy Joe Casserole

Ingredients

For the Casserole:

- 1 lb ground beef
- 1 small onion, chopped
- 1 (15 oz) can sloppy joe sauce
- 1 (16 oz) package elbow macaroni
- 1 cup shredded cheddar cheese (divided)
- 1 teaspoon garlic powder
- ½ teaspoon salt

Instructions

1. **Preheat Oven:** Preheat your oven to 350°F (175°C).
2. **Cook Pasta:** Cook the elbow macaroni according to package instructions; drain and set aside.
3. **Brown Meat:** In a skillet, cook the ground beef and onion over medium heat until browned. Drain excess fat.
4. **Mix Ingredients:** Stir in sloppy joe sauce, cooked macaroni, garlic powder, and salt. Mix well.
5. **Transfer to Baking Dish:** Pour the mixture into a greased 2-quart casserole dish and spread evenly.
6. **Add Topping:** Sprinkle half of the cheddar cheese on top.
7. **Bake:** Bake in the preheated oven for 25 minutes. Add remaining cheese and bake for an additional 5-10 minutes, or until cheese is melted.
8. **Serve:** Let it cool for a few minutes before serving. Enjoy!

Cabbage Roll Casserole

Ingredients

For the Casserole:

- 1 lb ground beef
- 1 small onion, chopped
- 1 cup cooked rice
- 1 head of cabbage, chopped
- 1 (15 oz) can diced tomatoes
- 1 (15 oz) can tomato sauce
- 1 teaspoon Italian seasoning
- ½ teaspoon salt
- ½ teaspoon pepper

Instructions

1. **Preheat Oven:** Preheat your oven to 350°F (175°C).
2. **Brown Meat:** In a skillet, cook the ground beef and onion until browned. Drain excess fat.
3. **Mix Ingredients:** In a large bowl, combine cooked beef, rice, cabbage, diced tomatoes, tomato sauce, Italian seasoning, salt, and pepper. Mix well.
4. **Transfer to Baking Dish:** Pour the mixture into a greased 2-quart casserole dish and spread evenly.
5. **Bake:** Cover with foil and bake for 45 minutes. Remove foil and bake for an additional 15 minutes, or until cabbage is tender.
6. **Serve:** Let it cool for a few minutes before serving. Enjoy!

Eggplant Parmesan Casserole

Ingredients

For the Casserole:

- 2 medium eggplants, sliced
- 1 (26 oz) jar marinara sauce
- 2 cups shredded mozzarella cheese (divided)
- 1 cup grated Parmesan cheese
- 1 teaspoon Italian seasoning
- ½ teaspoon salt
- ½ teaspoon black pepper

Instructions

1. **Preheat Oven:** Preheat your oven to 375°F (190°C).
2. **Prepare Eggplant:** Sprinkle eggplant slices with salt and let sit for 30 minutes to draw out moisture. Rinse and pat dry.
3. **Layer Ingredients:** In a greased 9x13-inch baking dish, spread a layer of marinara sauce, followed by a layer of eggplant, half of the mozzarella, and half of the Parmesan. Repeat layers, ending with marinara sauce and remaining cheeses on top.
4. **Bake:** Bake in the preheated oven for 35-40 minutes, or until the eggplant is tender and cheese is bubbly.
5. **Serve:** Let it cool for a few minutes before serving. Enjoy!

Pasta Primavera Casserole

Ingredients
For the Casserole:

- 1 lb pasta (penne or rotini)
- 2 cups mixed vegetables (bell peppers, zucchini, broccoli)
- 1 (15 oz) jar alfredo sauce
- 1 cup shredded mozzarella cheese (divided)
- ½ teaspoon Italian seasoning
- Salt and pepper to taste

Instructions

1. **Preheat Oven:** Preheat your oven to 350°F (175°C).
2. **Cook Pasta:** Cook the pasta according to package instructions; drain and set aside.
3. **Sauté Vegetables:** In a skillet, sauté mixed vegetables until tender.
4. **Mix Ingredients:** In a large bowl, combine cooked pasta, sautéed vegetables, alfredo sauce, Italian seasoning, salt, and pepper. Mix well.
5. **Transfer to Baking Dish:** Pour the mixture into a greased 2-quart casserole dish and spread evenly.
6. **Add Topping:** Sprinkle half of the mozzarella cheese on top.
7. **Bake:** Bake in the preheated oven for 25 minutes. Add remaining cheese and bake for an additional 5-10 minutes, or until cheese is melted and bubbly.
8. **Serve:** Let it cool for a few minutes before serving. Enjoy!

Cornbread Casserole

Ingredients

For the Casserole:

- 1 (8.5 oz) package cornbread mix
- 1 (15 oz) can creamed corn
- 1 cup sour cream
- ½ cup melted butter
- 1 cup shredded cheddar cheese

Instructions

1. **Preheat Oven:** Preheat your oven to 350°F (175°C).
2. **Mix Ingredients:** In a large bowl, combine cornbread mix, creamed corn, sour cream, melted butter, and half of the cheddar cheese. Mix well.
3. **Transfer to Baking Dish:** Pour the mixture into a greased 2-quart casserole dish and spread evenly.
4. **Add Topping:** Sprinkle remaining cheddar cheese on top.
5. **Bake:** Bake in the preheated oven for 30-35 minutes, or until golden and set.
6. **Serve:** Let it cool for a few minutes before serving. Enjoy!

Curry Chicken Casserole

Ingredients

For the Casserole:

- 3 cups cooked chicken, shredded
- 1 cup cooked rice
- 1 (15 oz) can coconut milk
- 2 tablespoons curry powder
- 1 cup frozen peas and carrots
- 1 cup shredded cheddar cheese (optional)

Instructions

1. **Preheat Oven:** Preheat your oven to 350°F (175°C).
2. **Mix Ingredients:** In a large bowl, combine shredded chicken, cooked rice, coconut milk, curry powder, peas, and carrots. Mix well.
3. **Transfer to Baking Dish:** Pour the mixture into a greased 2-quart casserole dish and spread evenly.
4. **Add Topping:** If desired, sprinkle cheddar cheese on top.
5. **Bake:** Bake in the preheated oven for 25-30 minutes, or until heated through.
6. **Serve:** Let it cool for a few minutes before serving. Enjoy!

French Onion Soup Casserole

Ingredients

For the Casserole:

- 4 large onions, thinly sliced
- 4 tablespoons butter
- 4 cups beef broth
- 1 teaspoon thyme
- 1 baguette, sliced
- 2 cups shredded Gruyère cheese (or mozzarella)
- Salt and pepper to taste

Instructions

1. **Preheat Oven:** Preheat your oven to 350°F (175°C).
2. **Cook Onions:** In a large skillet, melt butter over medium heat. Add onions and cook until caramelized, about 20-25 minutes.
3. **Add Broth and Seasoning:** Stir in beef broth, thyme, salt, and pepper. Simmer for 10 minutes.
4. **Layer Ingredients:** In a greased 2-quart casserole dish, layer half of the baguette slices, followed by half of the onion mixture. Sprinkle half of the cheese on top. Repeat layers.
5. **Bake:** Bake in the preheated oven for 20-25 minutes, or until cheese is melted and bubbly.
6. **Serve:** Let it cool for a few minutes before serving. Enjoy!

BBQ Chicken Casserole

Ingredients
For the Casserole:

- 3 cups cooked chicken, shredded
- 1 cup BBQ sauce
- 1 cup corn (fresh or frozen)
- 1 cup black beans, drained and rinsed
- 2 cups cooked rice
- 1 cup shredded cheddar cheese (divided)
- 1 teaspoon garlic powder

Instructions

1. **Preheat Oven:** Preheat your oven to 350°F (175°C).
2. **Mix Ingredients:** In a large bowl, combine shredded chicken, BBQ sauce, corn, black beans, cooked rice, garlic powder, and half of the cheddar cheese. Mix well.
3. **Transfer to Baking Dish:** Pour the mixture into a greased 2-quart casserole dish and spread evenly.
4. **Add Topping:** Sprinkle the remaining cheddar cheese on top.
5. **Bake:** Bake in the preheated oven for 25-30 minutes, or until hot and bubbly.
6. **Serve:** Let it cool for a few minutes before serving. Enjoy!

Cheesy Cauliflower Casserole

Ingredients

For the Casserole:

- 1 large head of cauliflower, cut into florets
- 1 cup sour cream
- 1 cup shredded cheddar cheese (divided)
- ½ cup grated Parmesan cheese
- 1 teaspoon garlic powder
- ½ teaspoon salt
- ½ teaspoon pepper

Instructions

1. **Preheat Oven:** Preheat your oven to 350°F (175°C).
2. **Steam Cauliflower:** Steam cauliflower florets until tender, about 5-7 minutes.
3. **Mix Ingredients:** In a large bowl, combine steamed cauliflower, sour cream, half of the cheddar cheese, Parmesan cheese, garlic powder, salt, and pepper. Mix well.
4. **Transfer to Baking Dish:** Pour the mixture into a greased 2-quart casserole dish and spread evenly.
5. **Add Topping:** Sprinkle the remaining cheddar cheese on top.
6. **Bake:** Bake in the preheated oven for 25-30 minutes, or until cheese is bubbly and golden.
7. **Serve:** Let it cool for a few minutes before serving. Enjoy!

Ham and Cheese Breakfast Casserole

Ingredients

For the Casserole:

- 6 large eggs
- 1 cup milk
- 2 cups diced ham
- 1 cup shredded cheddar cheese
- 2 cups cubed bread (white or whole wheat)
- ½ teaspoon salt
- ½ teaspoon pepper

Instructions

1. **Preheat Oven:** Preheat your oven to 350°F (175°C).
2. **Mix Ingredients:** In a large bowl, whisk together eggs, milk, salt, and pepper. Stir in diced ham, cubed bread, and half of the cheddar cheese.
3. **Transfer to Baking Dish:** Pour the mixture into a greased 9x13-inch baking dish and spread evenly.
4. **Add Topping:** Sprinkle the remaining cheddar cheese on top.
5. **Bake:** Bake in the preheated oven for 30-35 minutes, or until set and golden on top.
6. **Serve:** Let it cool for a few minutes before serving. Enjoy!

Creamy Mushroom Casserole

Ingredients

For the Casserole:

- 2 cups sliced mushrooms
- 1 (10.5 oz) can condensed cream of mushroom soup
- 1 cup sour cream
- 1 cup cooked rice
- 1 cup shredded mozzarella cheese (divided)
- 1 teaspoon garlic powder
- ½ teaspoon salt

Instructions

1. **Preheat Oven:** Preheat your oven to 350°F (175°C).
2. **Sauté Mushrooms:** In a skillet, sauté mushrooms until tender.
3. **Mix Ingredients:** In a large bowl, combine sautéed mushrooms, cream of mushroom soup, sour cream, cooked rice, garlic powder, and salt. Mix well.
4. **Transfer to Baking Dish:** Pour the mixture into a greased 2-quart casserole dish and spread evenly.
5. **Add Topping:** Sprinkle half of the mozzarella cheese on top.
6. **Bake:** Bake in the preheated oven for 25 minutes. Add remaining cheese and bake for an additional 5-10 minutes, or until cheese is melted and bubbly.
7. **Serve:** Let it cool for a few minutes before serving. Enjoy!

Zucchini and Tomato Casserole

Ingredients

For the Casserole:

- 2 medium zucchinis, sliced
- 2 cups diced tomatoes (canned or fresh)
- 1 cup shredded mozzarella cheese (divided)
- 1 small onion, chopped
- 2 cloves garlic, minced
- 1 teaspoon Italian seasoning
- Salt and pepper to taste

Instructions

1. **Preheat Oven:** Preheat your oven to 375°F (190°C).
2. **Sauté Vegetables:** In a skillet, sauté onions and garlic until soft. Add zucchini and cook until tender.
3. **Mix Ingredients:** In a large bowl, combine sautéed vegetables, diced tomatoes, Italian seasoning, salt, and pepper.
4. **Transfer to Baking Dish:** Pour the mixture into a greased 2-quart casserole dish and spread evenly.
5. **Add Topping:** Sprinkle half of the mozzarella cheese on top.
6. **Bake:** Bake in the preheated oven for 25 minutes. Add remaining cheese and bake for an additional 5-10 minutes, or until cheese is bubbly.
7. **Serve:** Let it cool for a few minutes before serving. Enjoy!

Stuffed Cabbage Casserole

Ingredients

For the Casserole:

- 1 lb ground beef
- 1 small onion, chopped
- 1 cup cooked rice
- 1 head of cabbage, chopped
- 1 (15 oz) can tomato sauce
- 1 (15 oz) can diced tomatoes
- 1 teaspoon Italian seasoning
- Salt and pepper to taste

Instructions

1. **Preheat Oven:** Preheat your oven to 350°F (175°C).
2. **Brown Meat:** In a skillet, cook the ground beef and onion until browned. Drain excess fat.
3. **Mix Ingredients:** In a large bowl, combine cooked beef, rice, chopped cabbage, tomato sauce, diced tomatoes, Italian seasoning, salt, and pepper. Mix well.
4. **Transfer to Baking Dish:** Pour the mixture into a greased 2-quart casserole dish and spread evenly.
5. **Bake:** Cover with foil and bake for 45 minutes. Remove foil and bake for an additional 15 minutes, or until cabbage is tender.
6. **Serve:** Let it cool for a few minutes before serving. Enjoy!

Mushroom and Rice Casserole

Ingredients

For the Casserole:

- 1 cup uncooked long-grain rice
- 2 cups vegetable broth
- 2 cups sliced mushrooms
- 1 small onion, chopped
- 1 cup sour cream
- 1 cup shredded cheddar cheese (divided)
- 1 teaspoon garlic powder

Instructions

1. **Preheat Oven:** Preheat your oven to 350°F (175°C).
2. **Sauté Mushrooms and Onion:** In a skillet, sauté mushrooms and onion until soft.
3. **Mix Ingredients:** In a large bowl, combine uncooked rice, vegetable broth, sautéed mushrooms and onion, sour cream, garlic powder, and half of the cheddar cheese. Mix well.
4. **Transfer to Baking Dish:** Pour the mixture into a greased 2-quart casserole dish and spread evenly.
5. **Add Topping:** Sprinkle the remaining cheddar cheese on top.
6. **Bake:** Bake in the preheated oven for 45-50 minutes, or until rice is cooked and cheese is bubbly.
7. **Serve:** Let it cool for a few minutes before serving. Enjoy!

Buffalo Chicken Casserole

Ingredients

For the Casserole:

- 3 cups cooked chicken, shredded
- 1 cup buffalo sauce
- 1 cup cream cheese, softened
- 1 cup shredded mozzarella cheese (divided)
- 1 cup cooked rice
- ½ cup chopped green onions

Instructions

1. **Preheat Oven:** Preheat your oven to 350°F (175°C).
2. **Mix Ingredients:** In a large bowl, combine shredded chicken, buffalo sauce, cream cheese, cooked rice, and half of the mozzarella cheese. Mix well.
3. **Transfer to Baking Dish:** Pour the mixture into a greased 2-quart casserole dish and spread evenly.
4. **Add Topping:** Sprinkle the remaining mozzarella cheese on top and add chopped green onions.
5. **Bake:** Bake in the preheated oven for 25-30 minutes, or until hot and bubbly.
6. **Serve:** Let it cool for a few minutes before serving. Enjoy!

Lentil and Vegetable Casserole

Ingredients
For the Casserole:

- 1 cup dried lentils, rinsed
- 2 cups vegetable broth
- 2 cups mixed vegetables (carrots, peas, corn)
- 1 small onion, chopped
- 2 cloves garlic, minced
- 1 teaspoon thyme
- ½ teaspoon salt
- ½ teaspoon pepper

Instructions

1. **Preheat Oven:** Preheat your oven to 350°F (175°C).
2. **Cook Lentils:** In a pot, combine lentils and vegetable broth; bring to a boil. Reduce heat and simmer for 20-25 minutes until tender.
3. **Sauté Vegetables:** In a skillet, sauté onion and garlic until soft. Add mixed vegetables and cook for an additional 5 minutes.
4. **Mix Ingredients:** In a large bowl, combine cooked lentils, sautéed vegetables, thyme, salt, and pepper. Mix well.
5. **Transfer to Baking Dish:** Pour the mixture into a greased 2-quart casserole dish and spread evenly.
6. **Bake:** Bake in the preheated oven for 25-30 minutes.
7. **Serve:** Let it cool for a few minutes before serving. Enjoy!

Chili Cheese Dog Casserole

Ingredients

For the Casserole:

- 4 hot dogs, sliced
- 1 (15 oz) can chili
- 1 cup shredded cheddar cheese (divided)
- 1 (8 oz) package crescent roll dough
- 1 teaspoon onion powder

Instructions

1. **Preheat Oven:** Preheat your oven to 375°F (190°C).
2. **Mix Ingredients:** In a bowl, combine sliced hot dogs, chili, onion powder, and half of the cheddar cheese.
3. **Transfer to Baking Dish:** Spread the crescent roll dough in a greased 9x13-inch baking dish.
4. **Add Chili Mixture:** Pour the hot dog and chili mixture over the dough.
5. **Add Topping:** Sprinkle the remaining cheddar cheese on top.
6. **Bake:** Bake in the preheated oven for 20-25 minutes, or until the dough is golden brown.
7. **Serve:** Let it cool for a few minutes before serving. Enjoy!

Southwestern Quinoa Casserole

Ingredients

For the Casserole:

- 1 cup quinoa, rinsed
- 2 cups vegetable broth
- 1 can black beans, drained and rinsed
- 1 cup corn (fresh or frozen)
- 1 cup diced tomatoes
- 1 teaspoon chili powder
- 1 cup shredded cheese (cheddar or Monterey Jack)

Instructions

1. **Preheat Oven:** Preheat your oven to 350°F (175°C).
2. **Cook Quinoa:** In a pot, combine quinoa and vegetable broth; bring to a boil. Reduce heat and simmer for 15-20 minutes until liquid is absorbed.
3. **Mix Ingredients:** In a large bowl, combine cooked quinoa, black beans, corn, diced tomatoes, chili powder, and half of the cheese. Mix well.
4. **Transfer to Baking Dish:** Pour the mixture into a greased 2-quart casserole dish and spread evenly.
5. **Add Topping:** Sprinkle the remaining cheese on top.
6. **Bake:** Bake in the preheated oven for 25-30 minutes.
7. **Serve:** Let it cool for a few minutes before serving. Enjoy!

Meatball Casserole

Ingredients

For the Casserole:

- 1 lb frozen meatballs
- 2 cups marinara sauce
- 1 cup cooked pasta (penne or rotini)
- 1 cup shredded mozzarella cheese (divided)
- 1 teaspoon Italian seasoning

Instructions

1. **Preheat Oven:** Preheat your oven to 350°F (175°C).
2. **Mix Ingredients:** In a large bowl, combine frozen meatballs, marinara sauce, cooked pasta, and Italian seasoning.
3. **Transfer to Baking Dish:** Pour the mixture into a greased 2-quart casserole dish and spread evenly.
4. **Add Topping:** Sprinkle half of the mozzarella cheese on top.
5. **Bake:** Bake in the preheated oven for 30-35 minutes. Add remaining cheese and bake for an additional 5-10 minutes, or until cheese is bubbly.
6. **Serve:** Let it cool for a few minutes before serving. Enjoy!

Potato Topping Casserole

Ingredients

For the Casserole:

- 4 cups mashed potatoes (prepared)
- 1 cup cooked ground beef or turkey
- 1 (10.5 oz) can cream of mushroom soup
- 1 cup shredded cheese (cheddar or mozzarella)
- 1 teaspoon garlic powder
- ½ teaspoon salt

Instructions

1. **Preheat Oven:** Preheat your oven to 350°F (175°C).
2. **Mix Ingredients:** In a bowl, combine cooked ground meat, cream of mushroom soup, garlic powder, and salt.
3. **Transfer to Baking Dish:** Spread the meat mixture in a greased 2-quart casserole dish.
4. **Add Mashed Potatoes:** Spread the mashed potatoes evenly over the meat mixture.
5. **Add Topping:** Sprinkle cheese on top.
6. **Bake:** Bake in the preheated oven for 25-30 minutes, or until cheese is melted and the casserole is heated through.
7. **Serve:** Let it cool for a few minutes before serving. Enjoy!

Savory Breakfast Casserole

Ingredients

For the Casserole:

- 6 large eggs
- 1 cup milk
- 2 cups diced cooked sausage
- 1 cup shredded cheese (cheddar or mozzarella)
- 2 cups diced potatoes (or frozen hash browns)
- ½ teaspoon salt
- ½ teaspoon pepper

Instructions

1. **Preheat Oven:** Preheat your oven to 350°F (175°C).
2. **Mix Ingredients:** In a large bowl, whisk together eggs, milk, salt, and pepper. Stir in sausage, potatoes, and half of the cheese.
3. **Transfer to Baking Dish:** Pour the mixture into a greased 9x13-inch baking dish and spread evenly.
4. **Add Topping:** Sprinkle the remaining cheese on top.
5. **Bake:** Bake in the preheated oven for 30-35 minutes, or until set and golden on top.
6. **Serve:** Let it cool for a few minutes before serving. Enjoy!

Baked Ratatouille Casserole

Ingredients

For the Casserole:

- 1 eggplant, diced
- 2 zucchini, sliced
- 1 bell pepper, chopped
- 1 onion, chopped
- 2 cups diced tomatoes (canned or fresh)
- 2 cloves garlic, minced
- 1 teaspoon dried basil
- 1 teaspoon dried oregano
- 1 cup shredded mozzarella cheese (divided)
- Salt and pepper to taste

Instructions

1. **Preheat Oven:** Preheat your oven to 375°F (190°C).
2. **Sauté Vegetables:** In a large skillet, sauté eggplant, zucchini, bell pepper, onion, and garlic until softened.
3. **Mix Ingredients:** In a large bowl, combine sautéed vegetables, diced tomatoes, basil, oregano, salt, and pepper.
4. **Transfer to Baking Dish:** Pour the mixture into a greased 2-quart casserole dish and spread evenly.
5. **Add Topping:** Sprinkle half of the mozzarella cheese on top.
6. **Bake:** Bake in the preheated oven for 25 minutes. Add remaining cheese and bake for an additional 10-15 minutes, or until cheese is bubbly and golden.
7. **Serve:** Let it cool for a few minutes before serving. Enjoy!

Crab and Corn Casserole

Ingredients

For the Casserole:

- 2 cups lump crab meat, drained
- 1 (15 oz) can creamed corn
- 1 cup cornmeal
- 1 cup milk
- 1 cup shredded cheddar cheese (divided)
- 2 large eggs
- 1 teaspoon Old Bay seasoning

Instructions

1. **Preheat Oven:** Preheat your oven to 350°F (175°C).
2. **Mix Ingredients:** In a large bowl, combine crab meat, creamed corn, cornmeal, milk, eggs, Old Bay seasoning, and half of the cheddar cheese. Mix well.
3. **Transfer to Baking Dish:** Pour the mixture into a greased 2-quart casserole dish and spread evenly.
4. **Add Topping:** Sprinkle the remaining cheddar cheese on top.
5. **Bake:** Bake in the preheated oven for 30-35 minutes, or until set and golden.
6. **Serve:** Let it cool for a few minutes before serving. Enjoy!

Pasta Fagioli Casserole

Ingredients

For the Casserole:

- 2 cups cooked pasta (small shapes like ditalini or elbow)
- 1 (15 oz) can cannellini beans, drained and rinsed
- 2 cups vegetable broth
- 1 (15 oz) can diced tomatoes
- 1 small onion, chopped
- 2 cloves garlic, minced
- 1 teaspoon Italian seasoning
- 1 cup shredded mozzarella cheese (divided)

Instructions

1. **Preheat Oven:** Preheat your oven to 350°F (175°C).
2. **Sauté Vegetables:** In a skillet, sauté onion and garlic until soft.
3. **Mix Ingredients:** In a large bowl, combine cooked pasta, cannellini beans, vegetable broth, diced tomatoes, Italian seasoning, and half of the mozzarella cheese. Mix well.
4. **Transfer to Baking Dish:** Pour the mixture into a greased 2-quart casserole dish and spread evenly.
5. **Add Topping:** Sprinkle the remaining mozzarella cheese on top.
6. **Bake:** Bake in the preheated oven for 25-30 minutes, or until hot and bubbly.
7. **Serve:** Let it cool for a few minutes before serving. Enjoy!

Herbed Chicken and Potato Casserole

Ingredients

For the Casserole:

- 4 cups diced potatoes (fresh or frozen)
- 2 cups cooked chicken, shredded
- 1 cup cream of chicken soup
- 1 cup milk
- 1 teaspoon dried thyme
- 1 teaspoon garlic powder
- 1 cup shredded cheddar cheese (divided)
- Salt and pepper to taste

Instructions

1. **Preheat Oven:** Preheat your oven to 350°F (175°C).
2. **Mix Ingredients:** In a large bowl, combine diced potatoes, shredded chicken, cream of chicken soup, milk, thyme, garlic powder, salt, and pepper. Mix well.
3. **Transfer to Baking Dish:** Pour the mixture into a greased 2-quart casserole dish and spread evenly.
4. **Add Topping:** Sprinkle half of the cheddar cheese on top.
5. **Bake:** Bake in the preheated oven for 45-50 minutes, or until potatoes are tender. Add remaining cheese and bake for an additional 5-10 minutes, or until cheese is melted and bubbly.
6. **Serve:** Let it cool for a few minutes before serving. Enjoy!

Cranberry Chicken Casserole

Ingredients

For the Casserole:

- 4 cups cooked chicken, shredded
- 1 (15 oz) can cranberry sauce
- 1 cup cream of chicken soup
- 1 cup shredded cheddar cheese
- 1 cup cooked rice
- ½ cup chopped pecans (optional)

Instructions

1. **Preheat Oven:** Preheat your oven to 350°F (175°C).
2. **Mix Ingredients:** In a large bowl, combine shredded chicken, cranberry sauce, cream of chicken soup, cooked rice, and half of the cheddar cheese. Mix well.
3. **Transfer to Baking Dish:** Pour the mixture into a greased 2-quart casserole dish and spread evenly.
4. **Add Topping:** Sprinkle the remaining cheddar cheese and chopped pecans on top.
5. **Bake:** Bake in the preheated oven for 25-30 minutes, or until heated through and bubbly.
6. **Serve:** Let it cool for a few minutes before serving. Enjoy!

Crispy Tater Tot Casserole

Ingredients

For the Casserole:

- 1 lb ground beef
- 1 small onion, chopped
- 1 (10.5 oz) can cream of mushroom soup
- 1 cup frozen mixed vegetables
- 1 (32 oz) bag frozen tater tots
- 1 cup shredded cheddar cheese (divided)

Instructions

1. **Preheat Oven:** Preheat your oven to 350°F (175°C).
2. **Brown Meat:** In a skillet, cook ground beef and onion until browned; drain excess fat.
3. **Mix Ingredients:** In a large bowl, combine cooked beef, cream of mushroom soup, and mixed vegetables.
4. **Transfer to Baking Dish:** Pour the mixture into a greased 9x13-inch baking dish and spread evenly.
5. **Add Topping:** Arrange tater tots on top and sprinkle half of the cheddar cheese.
6. **Bake:** Bake in the preheated oven for 30 minutes. Add remaining cheese and bake for an additional 10 minutes, or until cheese is melted and tater tots are crispy.
7. **Serve:** Let it cool for a few minutes before serving. Enjoy!

Bacon and Egg Casserole

Ingredients

For the Casserole:

- 6 large eggs
- 1 cup milk
- 1 cup cooked bacon, chopped
- 1 cup shredded cheese (cheddar or mozzarella)
- 2 cups cubed bread (white or whole wheat)
- ½ teaspoon salt
- ½ teaspoon pepper

Instructions

1. **Preheat Oven:** Preheat your oven to 350°F (175°C).
2. **Mix Ingredients:** In a large bowl, whisk together eggs, milk, salt, and pepper. Stir in chopped bacon, cubed bread, and half of the cheese.
3. **Transfer to Baking Dish:** Pour the mixture into a greased 9x13-inch baking dish and spread evenly.
4. **Add Topping:** Sprinkle the remaining cheese on top.
5. **Bake:** Bake in the preheated oven for 30-35 minutes, or until set and golden on top.
6. **Serve:** Let it cool for a few minutes before serving. Enjoy!

Mediterranean Vegetable Casserole

Ingredients

For the Casserole:

- 1 zucchini, sliced
- 1 bell pepper, chopped
- 1 eggplant, diced
- 1 cup cherry tomatoes, halved
- 1 small onion, chopped
- 2 cloves garlic, minced
- 1 teaspoon dried oregano
- 1 cup feta cheese, crumbled
- 1 cup shredded mozzarella cheese

Instructions

1. **Preheat Oven:** Preheat your oven to 375°F (190°C).
2. **Sauté Vegetables:** In a large skillet, sauté zucchini, bell pepper, eggplant, onion, and garlic until softened.
3. **Mix Ingredients:** In a large bowl, combine sautéed vegetables, cherry tomatoes, oregano, and half of the feta cheese.
4. **Transfer to Baking Dish:** Pour the mixture into a greased 2-quart casserole dish and spread evenly.
5. **Add Topping:** Sprinkle the remaining feta and mozzarella cheese on top.
6. **Bake:** Bake in the preheated oven for 25-30 minutes, or until cheese is bubbly and golden.
7. **Serve:** Let it cool for a few minutes before serving. Enjoy!

www.ingramcontent.com/pod-product-compliance
Lightning Source LLC
LaVergne TN
LVHW081332060526
838201LV00055B/2607